THE BRIEF HISTORY OF AKAL TAKHT

ISHWAR SINGH

Copyright © Ishwar Singh
All Rights Reserved.

This book has been published with all efforts taken to make the material error-free after the consent of the author. However, the author and the publisher do not assume and hereby disclaim any liability to any party for any loss, damage, or disruption caused by errors or omissions, whether such errors or omissions result from negligence, accident, or any other cause.

While every effort has been made to avoid any mistake or omission, this publication is being sold on the condition and understanding that neither the author nor the publishers or printers would be liable in any manner to any person by reason of any mistake or omission in this publication or for any action taken or omitted to be taken or advice rendered or accepted on the basis of this work. For any defect in printing or binding the publishers will be liable only to replace the defective copy by another copy of this work then available.

I am dedicating this book to the great warriors of Sikhism.

Contents

Foreword

Ishwar Singh have more than ten years of experience in writing story books, sakhis of devotional saints and in research activities. He is a tremendous writer. He is doing excellent job by writing about **The Brief History of Akal Takht**. *He had shown very keen interest in the field of* **religious resources** *and other cultural issues.*

He is also a very excellent teacher and also having deep knowledge about the social science issues. I have always seen him working very hard for his various books. He just want to express about the Indian culture to our new generations in a simple and brief manner. I wish him all the very best for his new book.

Birinder Pal Kaur

Preface

This book is about the brief history of Akal Takht. The task behind to publish such content is to spread knowledge about the important institutions of the Sikh history among the new generation. In the schools, which are being organised by Sikh trusts, the students are just getting very limited knowledge about the Sikh institutions. This is just an effort to spread this brief information among new generations. I hope that you will like this book.

Acknowledgements

Writing a book is harder than I thought and more rewarding than I could have ever imagined. None of this would have been possible without my best friend, my teacher, my best motivator, my beloved mother Amarjit Kaur. She was the first who inspired me for my goals and taught me various subjects and created my interest specially in Social Sciences. She stood by me during every struggle and all my successes. Whatever I had achieved in my life it is due to my mother.

I'm eternally grateful to my father Pal Singh, who took in an extra mouth to feed when he didn't have to. He taught me discipline, tough love, manners, respect, and so much more that has helped me succeed in life. I truly have no idea where I'd be if he hadn't given me a roof over my head whom I desperately needed at that age.

To my father-in-law Narinder Singh for their moral support during the up and downs in my life. He taught me how to live positive even in the worst situations by sharing his personal experiances. He is the man who suggest me to write a book in your life because it will be your book by which you will be remembered in future.

To Dr. Davinder Singh, who never saw my age, my race, or my lack of formal education. He just saw a kid hungry to learn, hungry to grow, and hungry to succeed in teaching. He never stopped me; he only encouraged me.

Prologue

India is a country of huge cultural diversities. This diversity has its roots in the ancient and medieval period of the history. In present day life, every one is playing his role according to the role assingned by the nature. I have very much interest to explore various great places and cultural aspects of our Indian Society. So an idea came in my mind to explore the brief history of Akal Takht. I am writing this book for our younger generations so that when they will read this book, they must understand the sacrifices of our forefathers.

CHAPTER ONE

Introduction

The highest Sikh administrative institution is called Akal Takht, which translates to "Throne of the Immortal." Akal is another name for God and signifies "The Timeless One." Persian word "takht" implies a throne. In front of the causeway leading to the Golden Temple in Amritsar lies the majestic structure known as the Akal Takht. On June 15, 1606 (today observed on 2 July), Guru Hargobind created the Akal Takhat as the location from which the Sikh community's spiritual and material concerns could be addressed.

In the 17th and 18th centuries, it served as a political bulwark against the Mughal Emperors. In the 18th century, Ahmed Shah Abdali and Massa Rangar conducted a number of assaults against the Akal Takht and the Harimandir Sahib. In a contentious military action known as Operation Bluestar, the Indian Army damaged more than just the Akal Takhat's exterior on June 4, 1984. In addition to that, tanks were used to smash the structure's sanctity and reduce it to rubble.

The highest speaker for the Sikh Panth, the Jathedar of the Akal Takht is intended to be a spiritual figurehead free from any outside, politically motivated influences. Giani Harpreet Singh serves as jathedar at the moment.

CHAPTER TWO

Martyrdom of Guru Arjan Dev Ji

The compiler of the Adi Granth, Guru Arjan Dev ji, was detained and executed by torture on the Mughal Emperor Jehangir's orders two years after the Adi Granth was placed in the Harimandir Sahib. In his biography, Jehangir speaks of his intention to convert Guru Arjan Dev ji to Islam and his hostility to his religion. He claims that when Guru Arjan Dev ji took in his rebellious son Khusro, he was given the chance. Although some historians believe that sheltering Khusro was a political decision, Guru Arjan Dev ji's life does not lend itself to this interpretation.

According to legend, Guru Arjan Dev ji made a lot of enemies as a result of his success in reviving Sikhism as a new age religion. They made a concerted effort to damage Guru Ji, and they even complained to Akbar in an attempt to do so. His interests were spiritual, not political, and it was senseless to kill such a brilliant thinker. It handed Sikhism its first martyr and turned a non violent reform and reconciliation movement into the most aggressive group ever seen in India.

The Sikh mentality was deeply affected by this tragic turning point, which resulted in a rapid and acute understanding of the idea of martyrdom. It gave rise to the custom of the neighbourhood standing resolutely up against injustice and the whims of despotic rulers. Now, the Sikh sense of mission and purpose had a fresh, enduring dimension.

Guru Arjan Dev ji ordered his son to "sit fully armed on his throne and maintain an army" in his farewell message before he passed away, knowing that his death was imminent. That's exactly what Guru Hargobind did.

CHAPTER THREE

Foundation of Akal Takht

After the unfortunate demise of Guru Arjan Dev Ji in 1606, Guru Hargobind accepted the guruship. Guru Hargobind, who at the time was only eleven years old, is thought to have started the Sikh Panth's militarization process right away. At the ascension ceremony, the Guru made clear his intentions: instead of the ascetic seli, he would wear a sword belt with two swords signifying Miri and Piri, temporal and spiritual authority. He would also wear the ruler's aigrette on his turban. By adopting conventional symbols of suzerainty, Guru Hargobind ordered his Sikhs to offer horses and weapons rather than money.

The foundation of his army was a group of 52 bodyguards that he raised. 500 young people from the Majha (the nation between the Ravi and the Bias), the Doab (the nation between the Beas and the Satluj), and the Malwa nations came to him to enrol (comprises the portion of the Punjab formed by Patiala, Nabha, Jind, Faridkot, Firzopur and Ludhiana). Gatka, the Sikhs' martial arts, is credited with having been created by Guru Hargobind. It should come as no surprise that Guru Hargobind's architectural endeavours reflect his goals and character.

Guru Hargobind ji, Bhai Gurdas ji, and Baba Buddha ji all worked together to construct the original Akal Takht building. The platform was constructed without the help of any other people or artists. The guru's seat would serve the panth forever, according to Guru Ji. In defiance of Jehangir's royal decree that stated that only the Emperor himself might sit on a raised platform higher than three feet, Guru ji raised the height of the platform to twelve feet. Guru Hargobind would frequently sit on the elevated Takht platform in royal regalia and administer justice to all Sikh conflicts.

The Harimandir Sahib and the Akal Takhat were built side by side, with the Akal Takhat somewhat lower, signifying the necessity of seeking spiritual grace first. The everyday activities of Guru Hargobind alternately accentuated the throne platform with its assertion of temporal authority and declaration of sovereignty, as well as the shrine with its spiritual function and self-effacing architectural symbolism. The Guru began each day with devotion at the Harimandir Sahib; he then went on hunts in the late morning and granted audience from the Akal Takht in the afternoon; he then returned to the shrine for prayers and hymns in the evening; and at night, he and his followers went back to the Akal Takht to hear martial songs of valiant exploits.

Hukamnamas, or announcements of advice or explanation on any aspect of Sikh philosophy, are made from the Akal Takhat. Persons accused of violating religious law or engaging in behaviour harmful to Sikh interests or unity may be required to pay penance. It may publicly express its gratitude for exceptional services provided or sacrifices made by people who support Sikhism or the Sikhs. Notably, nobody is superior to the Akal Takht.

The Sarbat Khalsa once convened at the Akal Takht and made the decision to punish Maharaja Ranjit Singh for his misdeeds with a predetermined amount of lashes on his back. Ranjit Singh, the Gursikh, submitted to the rules and showed up at the Akal Takat to be reprimanded. However, the king received a severe fine instead of being physically punished.

The only thing that remained of the Akal Takhat's original site was a tall earthen mound that spanned a sizable open area where Guru Hargobind used to play as a youngster. According to legend, the Guru's first Takhat was a straight forward, 3.5-meter-high platform where he would sit like a king at court, surrounded by symbols of royalty like the canopy as well as the flywhisk, and carry out kingly duties like accepting petitions and dispensing justice.

The Akal Takht of today is a sizable, five-story modern building (3 of which were erected by Maharaja Ranjit Singh), with engraved marble, a gold-leafed dome, and no resemblance to Guru Hargobind's original Takht or pedestal. Recent restoration work, however, has revealed a layer of coloured lime plaster that may have been a component of the original Takht. The original Akal Takht was kept at a level lower than the shrine despite having a plinth that was significantly taller than the one of the Harimandir Sahib.

Traces of Old Lime Plaster

Akal Takht made by Guru Hargobind Ji

CHAPTER FOUR

Akal Takhat Martyrdom of 1984

On June 6, 1984, the Indian Army invaded the Golden Temple under the name Ghallugaara (Great Destruction), even putting its main battle tanks onto the Parikarma. Untold numbers of Sikhs were massacred, along with members of Sant Jarnail Singh Bhindranwale's armed group, innocent pilgrims, and Harmandir Sahib attendees. The Sikhs' highest authority building, the Akal Takhat, took the brunt of the onslaught and sustained significant damage. Numerous Sikh artefacts were destroyed by fire. Similar to how Guru Har Gobind's decision to build the Takht was influenced by Guru Arjan's martyrdom, the Takhat's grave destruction served to stir a spiritual nation that had been dormant.

As we commemorate the anniversary of the "Attack on the Harmandir Sahib and the Akal Takht," may it serve as a constant reminder of those who gave their lives to uphold and defend the Sikh Panth.

Akal Takht after Operation Blue Star

CHAPTER FIVE

Artifacts at Akal Takht

1. Sri Sahibs (swords) of Guru Hargobind Sahib that represented Miri and Piri

2. Sri Sahib (sword) of Guru Gobind Singh Ji

3. Sri Sahib (sword) of Baba Buddha Ji

4. Sri Sahib (sword) of Bhai Jaetha Ji

5. Sri Sahib Baba Karam Singh Ji Shaheed

6. Sri Sahib Bhai Uday Singh Ji, who was with Guru Gobind Singh Ji

7. Sri Sahib Bhai Bidhi Chand Ji

8. Dudhara Khanda (double-edged sword) of Baba Gurbakash Singh Ji Shaheed

9. Dudhara Khanda (double-edged sword) of Baba Deep Singh Ji

10. Dudhara Khanda of Baba Nodh Singh Ji Shaheed

11. Khadag Bhai Vachitar Singh Ji which weighed 10 Saer

12. Guru Hargobinds Sahib's "Guraj" weighing 16 saer. It was given to Dharamvir Jassa Singh by Matta Sundari

13. A sword like weapon belonging to Guru Hargobind Sahib Guru Hargobind Sahib's Katar

14. Baba Ajit Singh's Katar

15. Baba Jujhar Singh's Katar

16. Guru Hargobind Sahib's kirpan

17. Guru Hargobind's Paeshkabaj

18. Baba Deep Singh's Paeshkabaj

19. A sword like weapon of Baba Deep Singh Ji Shaheed

20. Pistol of Baba Deep Singh Ji Shaheed

21. Two arrows of Guru Gobind Singh each cxontaining one Toala of gold

22. Medium sized Khanda of Baba Deep Singh Ji

23. Two kirpans of Baba Deep Singh Ji

24. Two small Khandas of Baba Deep Singh Ji

25. Chakar Of Baba Deep Singh Ji

26. Small Chakar of Baba Deep Singh Ji

27. Baba Deep Singh Ji's chakar for head decoration

Display of Shastars at Akal Takht

www.ingramcontent.com/pod-product-compliance
Lightning Source LLC
Chambersburg PA
CBHW022044150726
47990CB00004B/1610